Basil Brush Boom Boom

Stop that Noise!

Basil

Bingo

Mortimer

Based on the original Basil Brush animations
Illustrated by Bill Ledger
Story adapted by Clare Robertson

Basil was sleeping.
A noise woke him up.

Basil got up.
"What was that noise?" he asked.

Bang!

It was Mortimer.

"Hello, Basil," said Mortimer.
"This is my new drum kit."

"Stop that noise!" said Basil.

"I like it," said Mortimer.
"Do you think it is a hit? Bang! Bang!"

"No, I do not like it!" said Basil.
Basil told Mortimer to stop playing.

But soon there was more noise.

It was Mortimer.

He was playing the piano.

"Hello, Basil," he said. "Is this better?"

"No," said Basil. "I still do not like it."

Plink Plonk!

Basil told Mortimer to stop playing.
"No more noise!" he said.

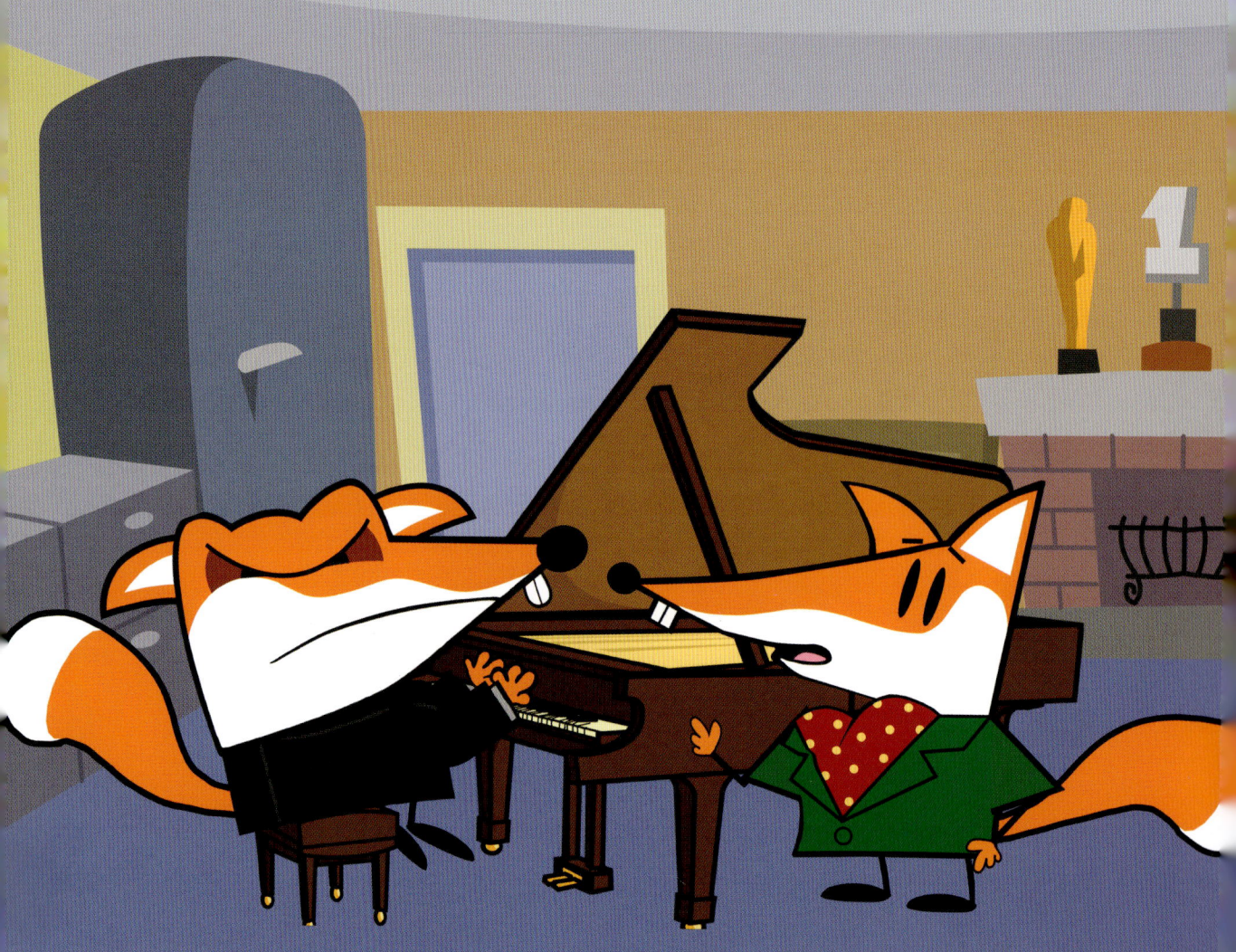

"All right, Basil," said Mortimer. "No more noise from me."
Mortimer was very grumpy.

The next day was Bingo's birthday.

"Look what Mortimer gave me," said Bingo.

"It's very big. What can it be?" asked Basil.

"Oh no!" said Basil. "More noise!"
"Bing! Bing!" said Bingo.

Boom!